Beowulf

Meghan Purvis received her MA in creative writing from the University of East Anglia in 2006, where she is currently finishing her PhD. Her work has appeared in publications such as *The Rialto, The Frogmore Papers* and *Magma*. She won the 2011 Times Stephen Spender Prize for an excerpt from her translation of *Beowulf;* another poem was commended. She lives in Cambridge.

Beowulf

Meghan Purvis

Penned in the Margins

LONDON

PUBLISHED BY PENNED IN THE MARGINS
Toynbee Studios, 28 Commercial Street, London E1 6AB
www.pennedinthemargins.co.uk

The right of Meghan Purvis to be identified as the author of this work has been asserted
by her in accordance with Section 77 of the Copyright, Designs and Patent Act 1988.

First published 2013

Printed in the United Kingdom by Bell & Bain Ltd.

ISBN
978-1-908058-14-0

ACKNOWLEDGEMENTS

More than anything, this is an acknowledgement of the teachers who shaped me as a writer: Patrick Farley and Bob Jost at Manchester G.A.T.E.; Steven Roesch and Jim Davis at Edison High School; Professors David Walker, David Young, Ronald Kahn, Dan Chaon, and Jennifer Bryan at Oberlin College; and Denise Riley, George Szirtes, and Professors Jean Boase-Beier and Clive Scott at the University of East Anglia. They made me a poet, and I am deeply in debt to them all.

I also want to thank the other writers I know who spent time workshopping, supporting, and kicking me along: Agnes Lehoczky, Amaan Hyder, Anna Selby, Benjamin Thompson, Hannah Jane Walker, Hayley Buckland, Hayley Green, James Brookes, Lev Rosen, Nathan Hamilton, Sarah Hesketh and Stephanie Garbutt. Special thanks to James Jarrett, who went to see the 2007 CGI film version of *Beowulf* at my request and still, for some reason, continues to acknowledge me in public. I would also like to thank Libby Morgan and the 2nd Air Division Memorial Library in Norwich, as well as Robina Pelham Burn and the Stephen Spender Trust. Both of them, in different ways, provided me with time and space to finish this translation, and it would not exist without them. Thanks also are due to Tom Chivers at Penned in the Margins, for his endless support and editing prowess.

And, finally, thanks to Heather Marzette Garner, Tiffani Marzette and the rest of their family; Mary and Rob Roellke and their family; and mine: my parents Jeffrey and Susan, my sisters Dara and Ellen, my brother-in-law Jeffrey Watts and my husband Luke Jefferson. Someday, I promise, I will stop talking about broadswords. Today is not that day.

PREFACE

I was in my third year of university when the professor of my History of the English Language class stood up at the front of the lecture hall and recited the opening of English's first epic poem. The hair on the back of my neck stood up —

> *Hwæt! We Gardena in geardagum,*
> *þeodcyninga, þrym gefrunon,*
> *hu ða æþelingas ellen fremedon.*

Not because of the language, although Old English does beat out a rhythm that makes one's hands itch for a pair of oars. Not because of the story — although, having read Seamus Heaney's translation the year before, I was aware of the power of this story of a hero's journey to do battle with something that changes them forever. It was because the class was taught by Professor Jennifer Bryan, and it was the first time I'd heard Old English spoken by a woman.

There were, of course, women already working with Old English and Old Norse: Marijane Osborn in America, Heather O'Donoghue in the United Kingdom, and others. But to a young woman still in university — even a good university, even one that often paid particular attention to under-represented voices — the idea that Beowulf was a story I could tell was a new horizon beckoning.

I realised later that *Beowulf* tends to attract translators who do not have their papers in order. Edwin Morgan was Scottish; Kevin Crossley-Holland discovered Anglo-Saxon literature after failing his first exams at Oxford; Heaney famously put a *bawn*, a symbol of Anglo-Irish oppression, into his rendering. My translation comes from writing as a woman — usually destined to pour mead and wait for the family feud to erupt — and as an

American. We have, all of us, snuck up to this poem while the gatekeepers were otherwise occupied. None of us came to this by birthright.

And in doing this we follow our source material entirely. Scyld Scefing was a foundling who rose to become a legendary king. Beowulf was never meant to rule: he fell into it by outliving everyone else in line for the throne. The world of the poem is populated by people meant for other things, and who wanted something different. They went looking, and found lives marked out by a beating poetic line. But they, the characters, and we, the translators, also brought things with us in our boats: a way of thinking about a building with sentry towers, a name of a Norse god, a sympathy for the women left to ferry pitchers.

My translation does some things with *Beowulf* that differ dramatically from the source text, most particularly in my approach to the structure: I have split the poem up into a collection-length series of poems that tell the story. By doing so, my translation makes space for the many voices within *Beowulf* that are often drowned out by a single narrator describing a single hero. This story is about Beowulf, yes; but it is also about the narrator of the poem, and about Modthryth and Hildeburh, about Grendel's mother, forever nameless. I have not given her a name, but I have given her and others more of a presence and, occasionally, a voice in the poem. Some people will say the shifts in focus and form I have made mean that this is not a translation. But my approach, like every approach to *Beowulf*, is still real; each is just as accurate as another, because translation happens in the space between, in what is passed over and what is held up to the light. Professor Bryan may have been telling a slightly different slant, but I listened, and now, over ten years later, I am telling my story of *Beowulf*.

I can't tell you what you will find in this poem. I can tell you what I've seen: boats splitting water, an arm underneath an ashen shield, something stirring in the night. All of it is true. But what you will hear — what *Beowulf* will show you, will lean to whisper in your ear — is something belonging only to you. Listen. You haven't heard this one before.

For my parents, Jeffrey and Susan,
for my sisters, Dara and Ellen,
and for my husband Luke:
for everything.

Beowulf

Beowulf

Prologue

HWÆT

           Stop me
if you've heard this one before: the lands up north,
hoar-bent, frost-locked, need deeper plows
to dig them. Here is one.

SCYLD SCEFING

This is a story about coming and going. This is a story about the sea.
SCYLD came in with the first morning tide, lightly carried
in spite of the treasures in his boat — mailcoats, gold, gifts
the color of water at dawn — rich omens, indeed,
for a baby still too weak to close a fist. At that age,
all palms lie open — an orphan's, a foundling's or a king's.

In time, his hand hardened into one we knelt to as king —
all of us; from the ocean he came in on to the farther sea.
I was gathering kelp when we found him, my back unbent by age,
holding his squalling face in the hollow of my neck as we carried
him to the hall, that first grey morning. I was repaid for that deed —
a small one, but one he was grateful for, if this lifetime of gifts

is any indication. We were lordless, in need, and he was a gifted
child — he took to his role of foster-lord, of king-in-training,
easily. Eager to have what was his, deeds
came quickly — he knew his way with a sword in his hand, a seabird
catching that first smell of salt. As his shoulders widened to carry
them, more and more retainers came — he marked his age

in men, not years; a loadbearer in a burdensome age.
Some he won over with gold, tracts of land gift-wrapped
in rainfall that followed the line of his eye. Some lay still, carried
off the field, the first and last tithing for a king.
I saw lifetimes of conquering and harvest, things I will not see

again. We have diminished, we are fallen — my one true deed,

performed again, taking him back to the grey death
he came from. He died in his sleep, of old age —
his grip on the pommel finally slipping, back to the sea,
back to a wooden boat — I carved the nails — and the gifts
we shroud him with. Gifts for a king, more than kingly,
gold he couldn't at his strongest height have carried —

And let them go, past the sightline of mist, let the sea carry
his gold, his body, and his boat — wherever it may, indeed,
to whatever shining demons, whatever black-hooded kings
may care to take my people's tithing for an age
we had no right to. Finally, my strength and my will gives —
let the tide pull him out of my hands, if the sea,

if the sea's unseen coast must have him, must carry
him off. This was a gift, this is the weakness of an undeeded
man, this is an age dying. This was a good king.

SUCCESSION

The crown passes: from Scyld to BEOW, famous among men;
and to his son HEALFDANE, who ruled as long as he lived,
grey-haired and fierce under the Scylding's shield.
He woke four children to the world: HEOROGAR,
HROTHGAR, and HALGA THE GOOD; YRSE, the last,
sent off early to ONELA, to brighten that foreigner's bed.

The lineage runs like knots of a spine, like the swollen knuckles
of an aged woman by the fire.

Here is the story beginning.

Here are the words you want.

1

Grey Skies

BUILDINGS

Hrothgar built success in battles, honed his voice to be obeyed,
a sword-edge, a line on a map
a voice to be followed. His company turned into a band, a battalion,
a hall. His mind turned to it: the greatest hall we would ever hear of,
margins still smoldering, licking at the cross-hatches
the greatest hall for gift-giving,
the greatest hall.

The orders went out across his portion of the earth,
to adorn the dwelling. And early in Hrothgar's time, the roof towered:
it was ready. He named it, HEOROT, a brandishing of roof-beams,
eaves uncurling to pointing wooden horns.
He said it, and it was done. A feast and a fire inside,
feasting, treasure given out: gold at its own tail.

The wide-gabled hall swallowed the sound, waiting for flames
that must come, that are coming, that came:
in the darkness the demon waited, miserable,
laughter spitting from the hall's mouth.
Guts of a harp were pulled, a poet's clear song to the night:

Who made this hall we stand in?
Who made the earth we tamp beneath our feet?
Who made the sun and the moon?
Who made what they illuminate?
And who knows enough to call them

what they are? Who knows the score?

The demon watched this;
the demon waited.

GRENDEL

1

Up the borders,
up the moors,
lie the bones
of mine and yours.

Comes in darkness,
comes at night
to find you out,
to claw and bite.

2

There is a delta of blood trickling out of Cain. Here are its eddies:
giants fled to the groundrock of mountains; elves cold as spring water,

their eyes blink irisless from the middle of the stream. Spirits,
bodiless, leading poor farmers and shepherd boys out into the swamps,

are here. All of them clutching rushes and snarling at God.
He is here, though I will not name him. The paper is burned out.

3

Border-wanderer, heath-walker. The line
is crossed. *Se* the *moras* hold —
se grimma gæst, mearc-stapa.

THE MOOR-STEPPER COMES

At night, with the brave Ring-Danes settled in
after their feasting, he sought them out,
their bodies heavy with sleep, oblivious to sorrow.
GRENDEL was ready.
He seized thirty men and fled with their bodies,
back to the darkness of death's house.
The sun glinted red off the walls,
a new sob-song of morning.
The famous chief sat joyless,
sorrowing for his men, for the traces
they left: blood in linen, torn-off nails,
clumps of hair on the doorjamb.

That night, he came again.

After that, it was easy to find men at a distance:
tucked next to cradles, pillowed in with livestock,
Heorot's belly sat empty.
Grendel fought with them all, the best house
stood hollowed and alone. Word of what they suffered
passed so far the word for it was different: *bana,*
bone, bane. Grendel conquered and was conquering,
a feud that would not end. A feud survivor, or a scorned man
we could buy off, but not him — for Grendel and for us
there were no reparations; the dark one sat in shadow.
None knew where he came from

or where he went. Dawn took him.
Night brought him back. Heorot's lease ran in darkness —
everything but the throne. Grendel left it,
wouldn't touch it. God knows why.

Our spirits broke. Men sat in council, considering strategies,
(*my kingdom for the mastery of this*)
how to barricade their minds against his terror.
Some promised sacrifices, blood-links
at heathen temples, praying that a bloodier god
would help in a bloodier time. They forgot God,
if they knew their Lord at all, forgot Heaven:
Hell in Heorot pushed everything else away.
Heaven forgive those who threw themselves into the fire,
who forgot our greatest comfort and hope, who could not change.
Hrothgar sat, brooding; there was no hero
to push these thoughts aside.
We had no respite: night covered all;
the things in the dark had won.

BAPTISMS

Stories of Grendel passed through boats and caravans — the currency
of gossip, hand over hand — until even Hygelac and his men
heard. His best thane (*and here you and I are on familiar territory,
here my story begins*) grew restless, grew eager

for the sea. A boat was prepared. We did not blame him for leaving us
to chase a folktale, a story on the wind — wisest and bravest of men,
we chose our champion long ago. We knew the omens.

He took fifteen men with him over the seas. The ship was on the waves,
passing under cliffs. The current curled sand back to the sea.
The ship was a swan, her neck foamed with saltwater. She swam

with nothing to glint off her bright arms but sky. Time and black water
swept the boat, until foreign cliffs appeared: a deadline, a full stop.
Mail clinked as the hull scraped on unfamiliar gravel. No one spoke.

We carried our swords out onto a glinting, sharp-edged shore
(thanking God for our safe passage). The sea-guard of the Scyldings
pressed his knees tight against his horse, waiting for the tide to talk.

TIDINGS COME IN

Who are you, who come mail-coated, soldiers dipped in steel,
across the sea? I see you — I watch for glints of armour
in a moonless night, rustle of longboats against pebbles. No one comes
like this — no one pulls their boat in, looking for a sentry,
polishing their shieldbosses in a noontime flush.
You're not raiders — that much is clear from your bright war-gear
and well-fed forms, from the span of your chief's shoulders.
But who are you, where are you from? — we don't trust outsiders,
and we've learned to fear strangers, so you'd better talk fast.

Their leader knew the correct response. He was raised right:
We are Geats, HYGELAC'S people. My father was called ECGTHEOW —
you may have heard of him; your king will have done so.
We come out of loyalty, if you want our help —
you can guess why we're here. We've heard of the hidden terror
that moves among your people, the mounting corpse-falls and blood-debts.
If I can help Hrothgar clear his house, I mean to.

The guard stayed on his horse, but his spear-arm relaxed.
Fine words, spoken well. I hope your works are as consistent.
I will take you to Hrothgar, you and your men; my troops here
will watch your ships, with their fresh tar tacky in the sun.
We will watch until you come back for them, come back to the sea.
Time will tell who earns his passage back to your homeland.

The anchors pulled and pushed in the breakers.

The forest fled before them, golden boar-crests
making their own way through the woods. The men hastened
until trees cleared; Heorot stood in daylight holding its breath.
Their guard didn't point out the hall. There was no need.
He turned his horse back towards the salt of the shore and spoke.
My bed is by the sea, thank God. I pray you protect this one.
I will guard your boats until you come for them.

The house-beams leaned in, vultures trading glances over a body.
The men marched with terrible swords and sea-weary shields,
wakening to the smell around them. The hall-door held no welcome,
guarded by men waiting, their faces to the woods.
One Dane watched as the men came near, picked out their leader,
and spoke. *Where are those shields from? I am Hrothgar's herald,*
and have never seen men with braver bearing approach our gates.
You look like you come more in boldness than banishment —
why have you sought us out?
The soldier answered from among the Geats, his face gone hard.
I sit at Hygelac's table. I would speak with your famous prince,
if he'll grant us the honor of approaching him.
WULFGAR responded. *I will ask the ring-dispenser about you*
and your petition. He passed to where Hrothgar sat,
old and very grey among his company, until he stood
before his lord's shoulder (he knew the customs).

A man asks to speak with you, my lord. I think I know
why he has come, and I think it would be worth your while
to find out what he has in mind. A fresh breeze
comes before you, from the Geats: he calls himself BEOWULF.

MEETINGS

I knew him when he was a boy; I knew his father.
I hear he has the strength of thirty men — quite a hand,
quite a blow behind it, and perhaps worth counting on.

Be well, Hrothgar! I am Hygelac's man;
I have done much in the time I've been given.
Stories of Grendel have reached my homeland:
stories of the best building on earth standing empty
and useless — and so Grendel's challenge comes to me.

Tell Beowulf to come here, and his men with him.
Tell him they are welcomed by the Danish people.

I told the wisest of my people I would come to you;
he knows my strength. He saw when I returned bloodied
from battle, covered in throat-gouts from five giants.
He knows of sea-monsters I slaughtered in blackening waves,
what I have done for him, what disputes my fist resolved, and now
I will settle this score with your demon. His card is marked.

I shall offer him treasure — enough to build a bridge between us.

I only ask that you give us a chance to cleanse Heorot.
I heard this monster fights unarmed — so I, too,
scorn weapons. We will settle this hand-to-hand,
trust the Lord to send who seems right into death.

If Grendel kills me, so be it — my men won't bother
bearing my corpse back over the waves, let breezes
carry the smell of my body over the sea. Grendel
can make a meal of me, for all I will care.
But send to Hygelac my best mail, if you can find it.
Fate moves as she must!

God has sent us a champion, a sign of His Grace
to stand among us. I have expected all this.

HROTHGAR'S WELCOME

So, Beowulf. You come to repay past favors
with a fight of your own. It may run in the family.

Your father fled here once, after he killed HEATHOLAF.
His own people refused to protect him; they were weak —
I mean no offense. He came, sea-mist clinging to him
after his desperate flight. My throne was still new wood.

Poor Heorogar, fresh in the ground — he was a better man
than I, but this youngster tried to fill his brother's boots.
We took your father in, sent boats heavy with gold
to the Wulfings, and your father's loyalty was mine.

I was a good man then, and strong. Now I am shamed,
and my crown with me. Grendel empties my hall,
my warriors fade away. Fate and the monster take them,
and God could prevent it — He sees all, hears our cries

and turns away. Somehow I pushed God from this place.
Night after night, men boast over great lakes of beer-cups
how they will stay the night, they and their broadswords
will haunt Heorot, waiting. Dawn lights an emptied room.

The walls stained and spattered, men missing,
the hall silent in the light.
Will you join our table,

scarred as it is? Tell us of the warriors in your time.

A bench is cleared for the Geats together.
Ale pours into cups. A voice is raised — a poet,
his song twisting through the night.

SOUNDINGS

Unferth: Hey — aren't you the Beowulf who swam with Breca,
the two of you risking your lives and your people's futures
on a bet? I heard your women cried on the cliff-top
trying to stop you, the peasants looked at their fields
left open, unfenced to the borders, and prayed.

But you couldn't be held back, paddling through winter's whelm
for seven nights, bravest and best leaders of men!
I heard Breca beat you, that you washed up on the wrong coast
limp and near-lifeless, tossed with the rest of the refuse
the sea tired of holding. If you can't even best water (he drains
his glass) I fear you may find Grendel too high a proof.

Beowulf: The more you drink, Unferth, the more you have to say.
Truth be told, I was stronger than Breca. We swam
with naked swords against what stirred from the seafloor.
Try as he might, Breca could not outdistance me, and I
chose to stay with him. We swam for five nights,
until the north wind turned against us, roughened the waves.

Shoals of fish swept my feet, the waves pulled; something
grabbed me, pulled me to the bottom. I stabbed without seeing,
rose for a breath, and fell again. So it went all night.
I was hardly the banquet the sea-monsters hoped for,
though I did provide the bottom with its share of meat.

By morning the shore was littered with sharp-finned corpses,
monsters I had never seen. They will not frighten sailors again.
Dawn brightened the headlands, the shores I landed on —
as you said. Fate often chooses to save a man
when his courage holds. Would that your brother
had been so lucky, before you gutted him.

Clever policy, though it won't negotiate you out of hell.
If only Grendel stood between you and your throne —
you never would have needed me. Instead he takes his pleasure
in the flesh of men, while you sit awash in ale and anger.
We'll see what morning brings after the feasting tonight!

APPROACHING TWILIGHT

It was again as before in the hall, with singing
and story-telling descants to clanking cups.
The gold-giver watched Beowulf and hoped.
At last Hrothgar grew tired — he felt the monster
closing in as the sun sank. Men rose;
Hrothgar and Beowulf nodded
as Hrothgar wished him mastery of the hall:

Since I was strong enough to lift my shield-hand,
I have never entrusted my house to another.
Now I leave it with you. Take it and, God willing,
hold it: think of the glory battle brings you
and look to your sword! Do not close your eyes.
Anything you want will be yours, if you survive.

Hrothgar and his men, and his wife WEALTHEOW
silent among them, went to safer beds in their camp,
left the hall to the Geats. One sentry stayed, watching
for the beast. Beowulf took off his iron shirt,
his helmet from his head, passed his sword
to his waiting attendant; before his bed he spoke:

I hear Grendel is fearsome indeed. So am I.
I won't kill him with my sword, though I could,
but since he knows nothing of sword-bite or skill
with steel, I'll fight fair. If he fights weaponless,

so will I, and may God grant victory
to he who claims the stronger hand.

The men went to bed impatient, eyes open above their pillows.
None of them, mouths stopped in the night, thought
he would see his home again — his wife's soft eyes,
the oak-grove he played in as a boy.
The evening's stories returned:
they sat where dead men once sat, they gulped mead
over their own graves. But the weaver of fate uses thread
that can wring a neck or warm it, and God
was on their side, ruling them as He rules us all.

GRENDEL COMES

Night came on. A walker crept in shadow across the ground.
The archer left to guard the horned building slept — as every night
for twelve years, guards slept, fled, disappeared. Who knows why?
Who knows how? The demon brought darkness, but he was awake
and angry, waiting the outcome of this battle swollen-hearted.

Grendel crossed from the moor, bearing God's anger,
coming to trap anyone left in the high hall. He came cloud-covered,
where gold plate decorating the eaves could be seen, glinting
on his battle-eager eyes. He had called upon Hrothgar's home
many times, but he had never received this welcome.

The bars inside Heorot's doors shrank back as he touched them,
his shoulders swelling to fill the doorframe. The fiend came
into the hall, toenails clicking on flagstones. His eyes
carried molten gold in their centers, burning in the darkness.
He counted the legion of men sleeping silently around the room,

measuring them all against the span of his hand, the space
in his gullet. He grabbed a sleeping soldier closest to him —
one bed away from Beowulf — and tore him apart, snapped
                              bone-links,
pulled at the knee cartilage with his teeth, mouth sucking for marrow.
He moved on, reached out towards the next bed with open claw —

but the bed grabbed back at him, a dark figure sat up.

Grendel had never felt a harder grip — he had been caught.
He tried to run, but the hand held fast. Beowulf thought of his promise
and stood, grip tightening, fingerbones popping, I could not
tell you whose. The monster wriggled, a landed fish;

Beowulf stepped into the turn, closing tighter. Grendel knew
he had made a mistake. The hall clattered with waking;
Heorot held clamor like a boiling stew-pot closed fast.
Danes in the darkness outside wept in terror at it,
at how Grendel must be slaughtering Geats where they slept.

Yell as he might, Grendel could not break free. Beowulf hacked
with his sword, (*the promise-giver breaks his promise, I hear you mutter,*
but what monster yields to mere words?) he and his men unknowing —
no weapon could hurt Grendel, no sharp edge or keen point
snap through the iron scales of his skin. The two careened
back and forth through Heorot, each hating the other.

A tear appeared: small, a shoulder-seam coming loose,
unraveling fibers of muscle and skin. Grendel's shoulder opened.
His arm unwound top to bottom, shoulder bones grinding
as cartilage gave way. He howled in hurt and terror,
his body changing into something painful and strange

at the hands of this hero. The last tag of skin broke,
and Beowulf was left holding an arm gone heavily slack,
collapsing onto the floor.
                          Grendel fled

                                        to the open fens,

back to his home,
                    air in his wound running
rivulets
            of a current: death,
                            death, death.

Darkness took him.

MORNING

The scraps of shoulder they placed under Heorot's vaulted roof,
along a beam braced above the throne. Men came in the morning

to wonder at it, to see bloody tracks leading into the hinterlands,
grass-blades smeared with blood, steps growing closer, deeper

as the monster faltered, muddy knee-hollows where he stumbled,
rousing himself to drag his body further. They followed him

to a mere, known for depths that concealed unknown monsters
and haunting mists. There was blood in the water. The waves churned,

full of knotting waterplants and gore. Somewhere beneath them,
Grendel lay. Hell would receive him. They turned back from the tide,

horses eager to return to their stables, old boys and younger men
flushed with a victory they would retell for the rest of their days.

They discussed what Beowulf had done: they agreed, over the earth
and under the sky's circuit, they couldn't think of a single man

worthier of bearing a shield. And they didn't blame Hrothgar —
certainly not, the gracious king! He couldn't protect his land,

but in all other things he was the model of a good king.
At times they raced their horses along the worn country paths;

other times a poet known for his word-hoard wrote a new song,
linking lines in a chain around a strong man, with a strong arm.

SCOP

If it's stories of SIGEMUND you're wanting,
I can tell you right now, we don't have enough ink.
I could speak until nightfall
with you scribbling away, and you wouldn't know

the half of it. Not that you'd believe me anyway —
between him and his nephew FITELA,
they got into enough battles to fill a history book,
laid eyes on enough wonders to fill a dictionary.

But his most famous deed — the one they still shout for
when the hall runs out of beer and over with boasting —
he did alone, under the earth. That was when he killed the dragon,
impaling it on a sword standing deep in the rockwall.

He earned the treasure he carried out of that place;
a ship low-waterlined with gold and bright rings,
the serpent burning behind him.
He was the champion we had prayed for,

growing stronger after HEREMOD's weakening,
when he was betrayed to the giants and killed.
That one brought sorrow to his people, grief to his thanes,
though only I am left to remember it now.

We had looked to our prince to save us, to protect

his land and his people. Beowulf is loved by all who know him,
but Heremod's hand fell heavy; his eye passed over
in a darkness that would not lift. I will not pass his story on.

THANKSGIVINGS BEGIN

When the men returned, midmorning light beamed on Heorot
as Hrothgar emerged from the women's chambers, to see
Grendel's remains for himself. He came up the steps with his queen,
looked at the hand, grey and dripping, under the high roof:

Thank God for this sight! Thank God my hall survives to hold it!
Through the Lord's might, Beowulf has performed a miracle
which our human wisdom could not contrive. Any woman who bears
such a man would say God was kind to her in childbearing.

Beowulf, I shall hold you as a son in my heart: anything you wish
within my power to grant, you shall have. I have given greater
to men who have performed far less. Your fame shall live
as long as your life lasts — may God reward your goodness

as He has rewarded mine! Beowulf flushed, and spoke:
It was a deed worth doing. You should have seen the monster,
encircled in his own arms, his muscles tiring, betraying him!
He meant to pin me into my own death-bed,

but he was the one trapped, as you can see in the rafters.
I wish I could have held him, kept him here whole,
but he was too eager to go. And he won't have any comfort
in his escape — he hasn't lived to fight another day.

Pain grips him now, and it will not loosen its hand

until his soul has gone to God's Judgment.
The warriors walked from their seats to where the hand hung,
inspecting pointed steel talons, spikes along the wiry forearm.

They decorated Heorot with fires and perfuming herbs,
gathered men and women for the feasting. The wall tapestries
shone with twisted gold, entwining fingers in the firelight.
The broken benches were thrown into the fire for kindling,

deep gouges in the walls that the decorations couldn't hide —
only Heorot's roof had survived the night's battle unscarred,
when Grendel turned and fled, the stain of death already blooming.
Fast as he fled, death had found him; he slept through this feast.

TALLY

We were rewarded, every one — treasures and heirlooms,
my fortune made in an evening of toasts. The best
went to Beowulf, a sword beyond price laid before him
with a helm and heavy corslet, a second skin of iron.

Who else could have done what we did? Who else
earned these gifts? A crown-guard wound with wire,
eight horses in plated bridles, feet lifting sharp and clean
off the brushed earth before Hrothgar's throne, as our drinking

drew on. And a leather pouch, heavy for the battle-friend lost
in the fight, set in the empty seat at our table.
There was no treachery by the Scyldings that night;
Heorot was filled with friends, gathered fast round their ring-giver.

Grendel bled gold. He would have killed us all, if not for God
and man's courage. He directed us that night, as He guides us still —
I clutched my gift-sword tight and thanked Him
for our leader's wisdom, for his cleverness.
We live through good and bad, if granted life enough.

THE HARPER

Wood and string sang out joyfully, and I
stood forth to speak. My song was for Wealtheow,
though none of the men in the hall knew it.

My song was of FINN's people, surprised and taken,
and how HNÆF of the Scyldings fell on a Frisian field.

HILDEBURH learned then to curse the Jutes and their honour:
she lost a son and a brother on that battlefield.
They both fell under spears, as fate demanded.

I sang for her, and for her sadness.

HILDEBURH

We were armies without arms.
Finn was too weak to drive us out
or fight HENGEST to the finish, and we
were tired, provisionless — we had to stay.

He swallowed the truce we tossed him:
Finn would empty us a hall, a throne
for Hengest to sit on, and Danes and Jutes
would own it and any treasure together.

Finn swore to it; Hengest made him.
He said those of us who survived
earned his respect, and none of his men
would be oath-breakers in word or deed,

or so much as complain. We smirked
to see Hengest settle into that second throne,
I can tell you. Then we buried our dead,
our old leader, Hildeburh's brother, among them.

Her whelp went on the fire as well,
she insisted on it. Flames lit the blood
staining their shirts, broken bodies bursting.
Fate does as it must. The fire took them.

We sat there, that slaughter-stained winter,

locked in sea-ice that wouldn't lift,
and those bastards sulking at our heels,
stinking faces I saw from under a shield.

Spring: but we exiles thought less of escape
than of vengeance, and when *Hunlafing*
brought battle-flame to Hengest, that warrior
took it up, and Finn fell in his own home.

The hall ran red, and our score lay silent
and settled. We looted Finn's house
and sailed with his woman back to Denmark.
We brought her back to her people.

They waited to burn our dead
until we were back in Denmark.
I sat in the boat, till they came for me
with welcoming garlands. My hair

smells of smoke. That long winter
and the smell of pine on the fire —
my husband smiling at me, my smile
and its stupidity, a mead-carrying fool,

my son in the flames. A handshake
sealed in blood, and I believed it:
surely this stalemate must bring peace?
Surely your word must be your bond?

Their new leader, on my brother's throne
in my husband's house; I am a spider
in a web of spun gold. I didn't gather wood
for the pyre; it would have been unseemly.

The light on their faces, hissing sounds
as blood leaked out into steam.
Heaven take them, watch over them both,
I was surrounded by snakes.

Needles through thread, pricked fingers
passing ale from throat to throat.
I was born to this. A bright smile,
weaving peace with barbing threads

that snap and slice. I saw their faces turn
and could do nothing. My hands fell empty
as they fought and fell, my eyes
in my murdered husband's face.

This house is gone. My hall stands silent,
this prow lashes me back to my home.
I am entombed in ice, I am frost-locked,
and what blood can open these bonds?

PEACE-WEAVING

The lay was sung to the end.
The minstrel put down his harp; games began again,
bench-noise brightened, and cup-bearers went forth with wine.

Wealtheow walked under her golden circlet to her two champions,
nephew and uncle. There was still peace then; they were still true.
Unferth sat at his lord's feet — his spirit remained admired,
even though he cheated his own kinsman in a fight. Wealtheow spoke.

Take this cup, my lord, and have joy in it.
Speak well to the Geats — be gracious with them,
and remember the gifts you've been given.
I hear you intend to make this warrior a son.
Heorot is clean, our ring-hall shines again —
be a generous giver, but leave your country
and your people to your own kind.

HROTHULF will treat our children with kindess
if you die before he does; he will repay his kinsmen well
if he remembers what we did for him when he was a boy.

She turned to where her sons sat, HRETHIC and HROTHMUND,
with Beowulf between them. She carried a cup to him,
inviting him to drink; she gave him two arm-torques afterwards,
a corslet and rings, and a great collar, a treasure from the earth.

I have never heard of a gift to equal that one —
not since HAMA carried off BROSINGA's necklace,
a shining jewel in its setting. He fled
from the clutches of EORMANRIC's hatred;
he chose a more permanent gain.

WEALTHEOW

Enjoy this collar, Beowulf, and make use of it.
Make a name for yourself with your strength.
Be a kind counsel. I remember you with this gift.

You have made such a name that men will remember you
as far as the sea surrounds the cliffs, where the winds rest.

Be blessed as long as you live; I wish you a wealth of treasure.
Be gentle in action, and joyful — here each warrior is true to the other.
Their minds are quiet, they remain loyal to their lord; these warriors
are united and ready. They drink well tonight; they will do as I ask.

Enjoy your wine, and when we go to our rest we will leave you
a hall spread with beds and pillows: sleep, in your greatest triumph.

THE COLLAR

Eagles hunt high. Their feathers glint gold against the sun,
mica among the loam-specks of crows a sky-current below.
They hunt by sight — a rabbit tensing to the ground, grass tenting
over a field-mouse's flight — or light against a gold collar,

a signal-fire gone wild to an empty sky. Coast closer.
The collar sits on Hygelac still, prideful where he clasped it
that dark morning, waves pushing him towards Frisia.
He fell under his shield, and his people's flag covers them both.

A hand covers the collar and the eagle loses interest,
Franks come for golden carrion once the bravery of battle is gone.
Hygelac's men sleep with him still, downed scarecrows
guarding a field of corpses. The wind has changed.

2

An Opening Sea

An Opening Sea

GRENDEL'S MOTHER

A man falls asleep, his bed beneath a hung shield of bright wood.
Who made it for him? Who will remember it after tonight?
He goes to sleep for the last time, brimful from feasting, glad

for his bed, his armor set above him, a scarecrow to the night.
Identical under a blanket to the rest, but not quite the same — he
                                                        squinted
when he laughed, he had a crooked thumb, but in a story set tight

with blood and bone, we forget these, we pare these things
away. This one would pay dearly for his beauty sleep,
for out in the dark, something of Grendel was waking.

His mother had met him at the end of his fleeing,
in the water-home Cain's mistake had left to them.
Grendel was torn apart, and she came looking for the meat

of her son, hanging from hooks in the ceiling.
Her home was a death-house, was becoming Grendel's tomb;
the hell-dam came — and was she less frightening

for being a woman? — hardly. The men in the dark room
screamed out that "he" was here, too caught in pain
and fear to see the claw at the end of an arm smooth

and hairless, sharp teeth in a softer jaw. There were drawn blades,

shields raised fast — helms sat watching, there was no time
for armor. She was quick — smart enough for a snatch-and-grab,

an eye for an eye, arm for long arm. She went to the night;
the man she carried made no sound. He was dear to Hrothgar —
a companion who had been with him for countless fights

and shared victories, now blood-remnants spattered
on what must surely be a deathbed. Don't look for Beowulf —
he is not here, he went to another bed after the treasures

at the feast. There was unending uproar in Heorot.
She had set a bloody brand under their old feud,
carried a beloved hand out to the crows and wolves.
Morning came blind and blinking, sorrow renewed.

WHEEL

I have never liked this kind of dealing, one bone
for another. The wise king looked about as if counting:
one day, his dearest thane was there, the next day gone,
time being counted out like knots along a backbone.
Troubles left, circled in the air, and returned.

HROTHGAR SUMMONS BEOWULF

Beowulf was fetched to the chamber in the full force of daylight.
He came to the hall with his troop, floor-timber creaking,
and asked if Hrothgar had spent a pleasant night,
blinking wide-eyed. He saw the grooves in the doorjamb.

Do not speak of joy in my presence; it slices my tongue
as I form the word. Sorrow has come back — ÆSCHERE,
my confidant and my counselor, is dead. We fought together
years ago, and the ringing of his sword against steel
has always sounded in the same key as mine.

Now he is slain — carried off, like so many before him,
and we thought the job was finished. We left the roots,
Beowulf, and they have returned — this is her handshake
in return for the one you gave her son. He fell in war
and the blow has come back — she has avenged him,
and now this debt hangs heavy round my neck.

WHERE TO HUNT

Out in the moors, past the town walls, we see such things —
the two border-walkers who keep the lost places. One is a woman,
or the form of one, one a man; and the two walk an exiled path,
a road scrubbed clean of righteousness. The male is called Grendel,
and I hope to God he has no brothers in barrows or badger-dens,
no father to complete their twisted family tree.

They live on slopes left to the wolves, grey headlands
where wind takes off the tree-tops and the mountain stream falls
into darkness, under the shadow of the cliffs. Not four miles from here
a mere lies in a rimed grove. A tree leans out over the water,
roots curling back on the hillside like whitening knuckles.

At night the lake drinks light from the stars: things grow blacker,
the water shimmers with a skin of fire. No man or child lives
who knows the paths along that riverbed. I have seen a stag
refuse to leap to safety — a bunch of its haunches, jumping
to ledges below, and my hounds would have gone hungry.

It turned from the edge, nostrils flared in terror,
and planted its hooves. Even with my dog at its neck it fell
where it stood, at the cliff's edge, for the rest to take.
The water from the lake stretches up in the wind, pulling at clouds,
the air is an ice-cold veil. The sky weeps: this is not a pleasant place,
but it is yours, Beowulf, if you come for that creature.

A SECOND FEAT

Choke back your tears, old man.
>*his contempt for weakness — the curse*
>*of a club foot, the betrayal of time*

We'll do better to avenge your friend
that to mourn him; a clenched fist
is manlier than a wiped eye.
>*we line up behind you, curling fingers*

Death comes to all of us, but a name
that lasts after death is the best bridge
to the next world we can hope for.

Let's follow the tracks. He
>*she, strong enough to kill*
>*your best man, and a woman*

will not escape into the brush,
or to a warren beneath the fields,
or into the trees — if the monster
stays *they stay, and us always*
with them on the seafloor,
we'll find him there.

THE TRACK TO THE MERE

The track was easy to follow — no footprints, no twin ruts
of dragged feet; the monster left a swath cut by bulk,
thistles at the path's edge capped with blood.

It stood out against the fens, a rope of scar tissue twisting
along an old man's back, following hills up into rocks,
a slope up to the cliff above a lake, an open mouth.

Their scout waited, white against a tree at the clifftop.
Æschere's head was next to him — hulled, discarded. Blood
wove below them, mist foaming and spitting at the troop.

The warriors' knees buckled at the view below: water-dragons
cleaving waves, leathery skin of serpents laid out on the rocks,
catching what sun they could from the grey sky. They turned,

puffing up at the war-horn's song. One soldier drew an arrow,
leaning over the cliff to give the muscle of his ash-bow room.
He hit a thing in the water low in its belly. Its fins flailed

and slowed; a strong wave rolled it onto a rock.
The men clenched their fists in revulsion: its swollen bulk,
snout crammed with teeth, blood leaking black into the lake.

Beowulf turned stonefaced to his chainmail, shaking it out,
war-cloth from a bloody clothesline. One of us helped put it on.

Its weight clung to him, bone- and breast-plate settling

next to each other, familiar. Next his helmet — he shook his head,
testing if the cap would stay on in the rush of water.
A boar along the helm-crest arched its back, defending

alike against Frisian sword-bite or a monster's maw.
Unferth watched and handed him his own sword, *Hrunting*:
iron-edged, blood-tempered, it had never failed any man in battle.

Who knows what was in his heart? Perhaps my suspicious eyes
sell him short, perhaps he gave Beowulf his luck open-handed.
But he was afraid to kick through the waves himself, and we knew it.

He lost face that day. Beowulf spoke: *Hrothgar, remember our words*
when Æshere's blood gleamed on your door. If I don't come back,
send Hygelac what gold you would have sent with me.

When he sees it spread out, he'll know what I've done for you;
he'll know what you are worth. Hrunting will point as my compass
towards whichever fate the Lord sees fit to send me.

After this performance, he leapt off the cliff — no pause for an answer
or wait for applause, though I know he expected it —
our prayers went with him anyway. The surge took him.

STONES BENEATH THE SEA

It was a day before he saw the bottom. (*Or did it merely feel*
like one to Beowulf? The sun's path was hidden to all that day,
under sky or under stone.) Before he turned his face from the seafloor,
the creature was upon him — the water echoed his movement
like humming strands of a web, and she came, pulling the water,
seeing who disturbed its weft. She grabbed him, nails ready
to slice eddies of crimson, drops of copper cordial,
but his mail held: he twisted against her, a steely crab in his war-shell,
her fingers stabbed uselessly. The she-beast dragged him
through the spindly water-plants that fed on sea-sunk offal,
leaves whipping in their wake; Beowulf couldn't draw his sword.

She broke through ranks of monsters — horned creatures,
rows of flippers, twisted bodies knotting in rage at the sight of him —
but bite as they may, his protection held. Before he knew it
they were in a hall, the air fetid, rocks scratched out for a ceiling,
and all of it lit by — *he turned his head.* Something gleamed in the
                                                                    dark.
Then she came, and all light blocked out in the grappling of bodies.
She swung an arm — Beowulf blocked with his battle-sword,
putting his weight into the swing. It should have cut her head in two,
thick-walled winter squash giving way to pulpy seeds within,
but the blow rang steel on steel, the blade twisted in his hand
like a tuning fork — the sword was useless. Beowulf let it drop.

And round the fire after, he told us he never thought of his safety

as the sword clattered away, disappeared into the darkness,
he just tossed away his sword. Giving up a useless weapon: how brave,
but I toasted with the rest and kept my mouth shut.

He grabbed at her hair, twisting it between his knuckles,
threw her to the ground. She sprang, grabbing with pointed fingers,
and as he stepped back his ankle turned — he stumbled, fell
on the rocky floor, and the creature saw her chance. She sat on him,
her knees weighted bags on his shoulders, stabbed at his chest
with a broad, bright dagger. She wanted to avenge her only son,
her only child, but Beowulf's corselet blocked her blade,
it would not let her in. Beowulf would have fallen to his end
deep under the earth, if it hadn't been for the war-mesh's help.
Beowulf wriggled like the fish he had fought, found his feet —
and found something else, too: an ancient sword, edge still gleaming,
a worthy weapon left from the time of giants. No normal man
could wield it — no man living but one.
It sprang to his hand,
the animals along the ornamented sword-hilt turning upwards,
as if they and their wielder were all gripping the blade. Beowulf,
holding the sword of long-dead ghosts, in a stone coffin
under the water, in the belly of the earth, turned
in what might be his burial mound, and swung.

The sword caught the monster hard on her neck, snapped it
with a noise like wire breaking. The tent-pole of her house
was broken; she fell to the floor. The sword shone red,
ice wrapped in rose petals, everything tipped in blood.
A light beckoned from the corner. Beowulf tensed,

sword across his chest like a benediction, ready to strike.
Grendel: greedy Grendel, man-devouring Grendel, lay on a bed
thick with marsh-leaves and filth, a husk among cattails
and reeds, the hole of his shoulder-knot towards Beowulf
like an open, beckoning palm. There was a debt to be paid.

Grendel's throat babbled silently as Beowulf took the head,
gave it the same answer as his arm. He dove into the water,
hilt and head in his hands. The water slowed, and stilled.
The creatures fled when they felt her death-throes.
The sea-cave's mouth was closed. I can tell you no more,
though I have seen it: there is no one left to speak for it now.

After he dove, we sat on the cliffside, watching the ripples calm,
then ripple again. The water changed: churning, boiling on itself,
growing dark with blood. I saw Hrothgar's mouth go slack,
I saw men move their eyes away, staring at the horizon.
He was a good man, they said. We would not see his like again.
We knew the woman in the water had taken him.
The air grew colder, settling. I saw Hrothgar leave, leaning on his men;
an old man. We sat under the exhaled lung of the sky, sick at heart.

The blood on the giant's sword sank in, eating at the metal,
salt on an iron hinge; the sword an icicle at the world-turn of spring,
melting, winter's chains falling away. Frost-bonds unlocked.
In the dying light from his sword, Beowulf saw treasures —
gold piled in corners, jewels left where they lay like rotten fruit.
He left them all — everything except Grendel's head
and the hilt that was left. The blade was gone, melted away

from forge-lines outwards, the hell-dam's venom
taking the iron with it in a final blow. It was enough.

Soon he was swimming: an upwards dive, water passing unchecked
through a sea barren of dark creatures, barren of life.
Beowulf made landfall with his cargo, the hilt heavy, head
already swelling with lake water. We ran to him then,
rejoicing in his body, dripping and unharmed.
We pulled off his armor, rivulets running back
to the lake, the water's face turned away, hidden
beneath clouds of staining blood. We went back with light spirits:
the country laid before us, orderly. The track was familiar.
Four men took Grendel's head on staves between them,
knotted him to it by his hair. We came to the hall,
brave in war and victory, Grendel's head dragging
along the floor, his cheek catching, cold and grey as a stone.

FOR HROTHGAR

Here is your prize, given with gladness. It didn't come easily.
Hrunting didn't help, but I found another weapon.
I killed the house-holder with it, and her blood
burned the blade away. I took the hilt and the head, slaughter
for slaughter. I promise you, you may sleep free from care
with your warriors, with your farmers and children —
nothing crawls dripping from the lakes for you;
blood has washed that road away.

A FOREIGN SCRIPT

The words spiralled down the hilt: can you read them?
They speak of an ancient battle, of water rising higher than giants,
of monsters falling in an onrush of water
the mountains could not hold. This was a cleansing.
The runes say for whom they were made, for whom the snakes
on the handle twisted, whom they hunger to serve.

HROTHGAR'S THANKS

This story will spread — people will retell it
as if it was their own, people will be proud of it.
Not like Heremod's feats for ECGWALA.

He was nothing to rejoice in. His growth
was no flowering, but a withering on the vine
that would not fail. He cut down companions,

each one falling to his harvest, until he turned
away from human joy alone, from his name,
from the strength God gave him above all others.

He lives on joyless, an affliction to his people.
You know this of course — you have virtues
of your own; I recite this story for you.

It's a wonder how God can give a man everything:
wisdom, land or lordship. He holds all the cards.
Sometimes one man gets everything,

a country in his fist. He lives in plenty —
not ageing, not ill, his compass points true,
with nothing wrong until arrogance turns inside him,

opens its eyes: death is near. It comes
at the head of an arrow burying deep, it comes at any time.

He owns too little, he can never own enough,

he hoards anger in the cave of his heart.
His gifts lie tangled and ungiven, and what's ordained
is forgotten and left to fall: he cannot share his honor.

It happens: the foundations of the body fall, the house crumbles.
We die. Cut down thickets of anger
where you find them, Beowulf, and choose better:

choose eternal rewards. Your strength follows the sun
in full flower, and it will for seasons. But things will turn:
illness, or sword's edge come;

a grasping mouth of fire, flood's unrelenting rush,
a ruined harvest; sword's bite, a spear on darting wings,
or failing these, old age

that withers and twists you, a light dying in your eyes.
It will come, dear Beowulf, and death will come
for you. This sky has seen me

a hundred half-years, war has watched me coming and fled.
But things turn: a scale shifts, a wheel's set in motion,
sorrow follows joy. Grendel came,

and his coming weighed upon me. Thank God
I have part of my life left to see him dead,
see his head dripping onto my floorboards. GOD IS GOOD.

REST

Night drew its cloak; warriors' faces grew dark.
The senior guard arose; Hrothgar, grey hair shining
in the moonlight, knew it was time to depart.

Beowulf wanted rest as well, went to his bower
travel- and battle-weary. He put his head
on foreign pillows, slept in a foreign house.

His dreams knotted his brow, but the place?
— night comes home and pulls her curtains tight,
I can see no more. The hall towered wide-gabled,
gold silent against the raven-wing of night.

LEAVETAKING

Morning came, light after shadow.
The men hastened, eager to be away,
Unferth with the rest. Beowulf thanked him,
said he couldn't be blamed for his failing sword.
(*That was a gallant warrior — getting one last dig.*)
And then, shields locked, ankle-braces tightened,
warriors followed their prince to the high seat.

Our homes are horizons away, our lord waits
for our return. If you have need again, I'll know —
if the waves pass tidings of your invasion,
if we hear foot-stamps of enemy soldiers against you,
I will be here with a thousand men. Hygelac will back me
in word and deed. If he comes to your court,
he will find friends here.
Hrothgar answered:
The Lord whispers words to your heart;
you speak them wisely. You are strong, in arm
and spirit. If a spear takes Hrethel's *son, or sickness*
leaves him cold and still in his castle, your people
could not do better than to replace him with you.
The Geats and Danes will live peacefully, one
by the other — no more bloodshed, as long as this hold
is mine. There will be treasures shared, and words
called over the seabirds' bathing-pool, curved hulls
bending to each other like embracing arms.

I know these people as I know you, and we are friends.

There was more treasure given, where we all could see it,
and the men kissed and embraced. Hrothgar's head dropped
onto Beowulf's shoulder; hidden, his face fell.
I feel it in my heart, that this is our last parting,
our last meeting: I will not live to see this man again.
Beowulf walked, proud in the gold he carried, proud
on the grass leading to the shore, proud in his youth,
his strength, his leaving. The boat rose, expectant, on anchor.

HROTHGAR'S REQUIEM

And why should we blame Hrothgar for his wet eyes,
for his weakness? He was a good king, blameless, until age
— that whisper in the ear, that tremor in the arm — began to tell him
that spring no longer flowered for him, that one day
frost would hold. He lost his strength, then, and in time his joy:
that sorrow comes for all of us, if we are lucky and live long.

SAIL

The men came to shore: high-spirited, the forest silent
beneath the sound of their voices, their armour creaking,
stamping of feet. The coastguard greeted them,
rode to welcome them back to the sea. Treasure stacked
on the broad sand: wargear with jewels and twisted wire,
horses with necks curved as the prow before them.
The boat-keeper was rewarded with a gold-bound sword;
the mast towered above Hrothgar's generous gifts.

The ship swept away. Sail-ropes for open water
lashed the mast, sea-wood groaned and creaked.
It sailed, foam bubbling at its throat, waves glinting
on prow-rings. They aimed for headlands, hiding in wait
beneath Geatish cliffs. Finally, wind thrust the keel onto sand,
the boat rested. The harbour-guard had been watching for them —
the broad-ribbed ship was moored to the sand, safe
from trouble-seeking waves.
The warriors carried treasures
to Hygelac, son of Hrethel, to their own hall by the sea-cliffs.
Their castle and king stood mighty, and their queen HYGD —
very young, but very gracious, even in her newness to the house.
Nor was she stingy with gifts, like MODTHRYTH.

MODTHRYTH

A woman hardens her gaze at a man staring soft-eyed.
At once he needs night air, or curls his shoulders over his belly,
struck — there was a time I could mouth her name to you
and we would nod into our cups. Now the name is unfamiliar.
I hesitate on it, tongue tasting an unfamiliar berry,

strange fruit. Let me tell the story again. Noble and terrible,
no one but her husband would dare approach her, for fear
they would be weight for a rope's end by nightfall.
How queenly is that, no matter how beautiful?
Born to be peace-weaver, then fills her country with death,

taking men's lives over nothing. But HEMMING's kin put a stop to that.
You'll hear, if you wait round the table, how Modthryth calmed
once she was given to a young champion, sent away
over the whale-paths to marry. There she was good,
and known for her goodness; she was a noble wife to OFFA,

the spear-brave king, who held his homeland.
From him came EOMER, Hemming's kin, grandson of GARMUND —
but you don't know these names either? You knew an Offa once —
no matter. I tell these stories because they are the ones
told to me; I plant my feet in the schoolroom and sing.

HOMECOMING

Beowulf set off with his companions along the shore,
the world's candle shining over them and the broad beach.

They came eagerly to where their champion, ONGENTHEOW's slayer,
shared out his rings. Hygelac had heard of Beowulf's return,

was waiting when he came — alive, unharmed — into the palace.
Hygelac ordered the floor cleared, a space made for Beowulf at his feet.

The survivor sat down with his king, after greeting him
with the ceremonial words — learnt by rote, of course,

but heartfelt. HÆRETH's daughter moved , passing mead-cups
with her caring hands. Hygelac began: *So. How did you fare, Beowulf,*

after you decided so suddenly to seek out distant battles at Heorot?
Are Hrothgar's problems solved? I've been worried,

riding a lake of my own sorrow's surges — I asked you, remember,
not to seek an evil spirit who doesn't know to count you as his enemy,

to let the Danes test themselves against Grendel's anger alone.
But let's not quarrel now: I thank God to see you back safe.

BEOWULF'S VERSION

What happened between me and those two monsters is no secret.
They made the Scyldings' lives a misery, but I avenged all that;
Grendel's kin does not live to boast of another dawn-clash with me.

Where to begin. I greeted Hrothgar — he remembered me well
as Healfdane's son, as a man worth knowing. I sat with his own son.
I wager I'll never be under a roof with such company again.

At times the queen, their bond of peace, passed, praising the men —
she gave a handful of torques out before she returned to her seat.
Sometimes Hrothgar's daughter, Freawaru, carried their cups.

She's promised to INGELD, FRODA's son — that's Hrothgar's doing.
He believes it will make their people friends, settle his share
of feuds and killing. But I don't know of anywhere that buries spears

with a slaying and lets them rest, no matter how good the bride.
The Heathobard lord will be as angry as the rest, to see a Dane walk in
with their woman on his arm, with their heirlooms on his chest.

Then an old warrior, a cup between his hands, sees the ring —
a man old enough to remember it and how it was lost,
how it was taken at a bloody spear-point — that's a grim memory

to hold alone, and he'll share it with a young champion at his side,
to test his spirit: *Maybe you, friend, recognise that sword as well —*

it's the one your father carried off to battle. His last, wasn't it? —

when Danes struck him down, took the sword after WITHERGYLD *fell,*
after the deaths of so many? Now some whelp walks exulting in it,
like a boot at your back, boasting of murder and bearing your treasure —

treasure that is rightfully yours. He whets the young man's mind with
words,
until their woman's man lies bloody-bearded for his father's battle,
a score balanced on a blade. The boy will escape, running and alive,
but the rest —

there will be oath-breaking and sword-clash; Ingeld will boil with hate.
Against that heat his love for his wife, his foreign beauty, will cool.
So the Heathobards' loyalty, their friendship — that will not count for
much.

But let me tell you about Grendel, my treasure-giver, so you'll know
what came afterwards. Once heaven's jewel crossed the earth, Grendel
sought us
where we waited, still whole, guarding the hall. Battle's hand came down:

HONDSCIO was the first to fall dead. Grendel ate him, swallowing the body
like a man swallows a pilchard. And he wasn't done; he would have left
full-bellied and empty-handed, but he wanted to test my strength.

His eager palm stretched towards me. Some kind of sack or bag
hung behind him strangely seamed, clasped with devil's skill and
dragon skin.

He would have tossed me in with the rest, but I grew angry, I stood up.

It would take too long to tell you how I paid him back for each killing,
each mouthful, but I brought you honor. He escaped to enjoy the dregs of
his sorry life,
but a trace of him remained — his hand in the beams, and he left
humbled.

I was rewarded as the Scyldings' most deadly friend, with plated gold
and treasure, when morning came and we sat down to the feast.
There were tales and songs. An old Scylding told stories from long ago,

sad and true, one night a strange story for their great-hearted king. The old
man cried
for his youth, his battle-strength long gone, his heart welling up.
We spent the day there, remembering and forgetting, until night came
again.

Then Grendel's mother, ready for revenge, set on her sorrowful journey.
Her son died in battle with the Wedras. The monstrous woman got her
own back —
one man was slaughtered. Æschere, Hrothgar's counselor — she snuffed
him out,

a vanishing light. That terrible morning we couldn't burn him, death-
weary at dawn,
no fire to spark or pyre to put him on; his body was carried off, a fiend's
embrace
in the dark under a mountain. That was Hrothgar's greatest sorrow.

The prince begged me to make a battlefield of the seabed, to risk my life
in a press of water for a full reward. And I did it: I dove in, and now it is
known
far and wide that I found the guardian of the deep. We fought hand-to-
hand,
the lake's blood boiling, and at last I chopped off the head of Grendel's
mother
with her own gigantic blade. I wasn't yet fated to die. They gave me more
treasure —
Hrothgar is in all things good and generous — and now I bring them to
you.

I depend on you, Hygelac; I have little kin, and only one lord.
Hrothgar gave all this to me, and begged me to tell you this story:
Heorogar had it, and passed it to Heoroweard, loyal though he was.
Without your grace I am nothing, and so it passes to you.

GIFT-GIVING

Let me tell you what happened next. We brought in four horses,
stamping and snorting, apple-dark in the hall. He gave them willingly,
with an open hand — no strings attached, no knots; just faith, sure
and strong in himself and in the strength of his companions.

I heard Hygd had the neck-ring Wealtheow gifted, with three horses
sleek under bright saddles. We thought well of Ecgtheow's son then —
his deeds were famous, he walked tall and sure in glory.
He never struck at friends or strangers with empty tankards,

he did not have a savage heart. Oh, he's quite the hero now, but I know
his tough time of it, still green, when I heard him called a coward,
when the court would say full-voiced how he was lazy and slow.
But a change came on him, a wheel turned; his glory flowered.

Then Hygelac had Hrethel's heirloom brought out; a finer sword
than the one laid across Beowulf's lap was never shown.
He was given a harvest-full of land, a hall and throne.
They had right to it: one above another, and our kingdom under both.

The sun spun in the heavens, faces turned. In the crash of battle
Hygelac fell, and his son HEARDRED cut out from the shield-wall.
Next they came for HERERIC's nephew — that time looms black
and dripping; I will not speak of it. Finally the land and hall
were Beowulf's alone. He kept it fifty winters, frost after sun,
until we all were prosperous, and happy, and old. Sorrow turned.

3

Smoke Rising

THE DRAGON

This is an unknown door. We should not be here.
In dark of night, a dragon rules *is ruling, will rule*
a hoard in a barrow-hall, we cannot be here, the pen
in my hand shakes, I cannot write. The pen is a treasure
that burns — was I reaching? There is no light here,
I cannot see. I took in my hand

           what is in my hand, He will   this,
he will come when he wakes and sees our trickery,
every household will know in its beams and bones
we have angered it. Who do we blame? A kinsman *a slave*
fleeing *the page spits my story back at me*, homeless,
finding a door we have no name for: *mwatīde*, it means nothing.

        Fear goes there. That is all.
The thing rises

          we have never been here, for god's sake
don't look

         fear overcomes him,
a space opens, he takes it.

THE BARROW

There are many of these houses in the earth — built for men from days
passed out of the memory-house, names we no longer know,
who hid their treasures in the earth. Death carried them away,
until the last left — most faithful, most lonely, of all men most alone —

felt the earth turning, and knew the dark eyes opening upon him.
His barrow stood ready on the headland, stood by the sea.
His arms finally empty, the man spoke: *Earth, hold what men
cannot, our gear welcomes your grasp! My people are carried off.*

The hall that held their shouts lies still, its mouth has stopped.
No hands grasp a sword, no lips pull from plated cup. Men
who made these things are gone. The burning helmet has lost
its best ornament; the battle-mask shuts its eyes; coats that held

against sword-bite and spear-thrust unweave themselves
and decay. The harp plucked in joy is silent, horse's hooves
strike happier courtyards I cannot see. The hawk that swept
through our hall is gone, passed into outer darkness.

He spoke in sorrow and was gone. No one can say when,
or where, or who he was, when death finally found him.

THE WHEEL TURNS

Something found joy in it:
a ravager saw it open to the sky, filled the cave with flame,
flying in a night enfolded in fire. He guarded his hoard
for three hundred years, until an unlucky man enraged him,
unlocked the spring. The man returned to his master,
his trembling palm filled with gold, a cup's open mouth
saying peace, peace. The hoard was found
and raided, and his unhappy wish was granted.
The treasure stood unveiled and ancient under the sky.
The dragon woke. He slid along stone, he found the faintest traces
of a desperate, wheedling foot-fall, hugging stone walls,
close enough to warm his heels on dragon-breath. (*And here is one
graced by god: Daniel in the dragons' den.*) The hoard-guard searched,
sniffing out their paths, circling his barrow furious and fire-hearted.
He twisted and turned — the cup became the only cup,
the only cup in the world — everything stank of men, of tampering,
and night could not come soon enough. Daylight failed
and the dragon went forth in flame.

There was joy in his breath,
in his horrible exhaling — he burned everything before him.
People screamed at their bright houses burning, at the earth
baking helpless beneath them. He left nothing alive.
At dawn he returned to his barrow, happy and hated;
the belt he tied around the Geats smoldered in its own ash.

News was brought to Beowulf — the monster threatening his people,

burning his own hall, twisted like wax into bright fire and nothingness.
He mourned it. Beowulf feared he had angered God, he had broken
an ancient and unknown law; the champion worried at his own doubt.

His hall was lost to the dragon; the land burnt out to the sea.
The king fought back against despair, and prepared his revenge.
He ordered a curious shield made, forged entirely from iron —
he knew the forest could not help him; linden-wood
would not hold against flame. (*The metal, tempered in fire,*
singing out a new age, and the two deaths required to bring it.
Beowulf, we sing for you, through voices choked with soot.)

Beowulf turned from his people — no troops to track the dragon,
no army massed against it. He chose single combat, as he always did,
for he had been in tight spots. He knew the narrow places of the world:
what arm could match his own?

                    I saw Hygelac fall,
struck down in the bloodbath of Frisia. Beowulf escaped by water,
swam for his life: he carried the armor of thirty men along with him.
Few who shouldered shields against him
could hope to return home. Beowulf, sad and alone,
returned to his people. Hygd offered him heirlooms,
the throne itself — sick at heart, she knew her son could not hold it
with Hygelac gone. He refused and stood at Heardred's right hand,
ready and respectful until Heardred was old enough,
manly enough, to rule his people himself.

Two exiles, OTHERE's sons, came out of the sea;

they rebelled against their ruler, the best of the sea-kings.
Heardred received them, and through them his own death;
he lay lifeless in his own hall for his hospitality.
Heardred dead, Onela sailed home again, leaving the throne
to Beowulf; THERE WAS A GOOD KING.
                              Beowulf waited;
his help came slowly, but sure-footed: the other son,
unhappy EADGILS, was sent weapons and warriors over open sea.
Onela fell in his vengeance. Beowulf and his people were satisfied.

And so it went: Beowulf outlasted blood-feuds and battles,
until the dragon came. He set out with eleven men
in search of the serpent. By then the cup had come to him,
and the holder with it — cowering and cowardly, the thirteenth man,
guiding them to a cave by the fretting sea. Inside, the dragon,
waiting, watching; eager for a bargain to be struck.

Beowulf rested on the headland, feeling fate approach,
restless and ready for death. His body's clasps were loosening,
his soul growing pinions, preparing for flight.

BEOWULF'S INVENTORY

I have seen times like these. I was seven when Hrethel received me
from my father, protected and loved me like his own boys; HEREBALD,
HÆTHCYN, and my own Hygelac. Herebald's death was wrong —

at his brother's hand, a terrible accident. A bent bow, a wide shot,
and Herebald struck down by Hæthcyn: a crime without criminals,

an accidental murder. How would one avenge it?
We mourned like a man living too long, lived
to see his son ride young on the gallows.

He sings an elegy as his son hangs, food for ravens,
and he cannot help him, old and wise as he is,
cannot do anything. Each sunrise reminds him

his son journeys beyond his reach; a second son
is useless in his father's hall. He wanders
through the orphaned hold, a home for wind;
horsemen sleep in their graves.

The harp lays un-sounded; there is no happiness there.
Alone, he goes to bed with his grief. Everything
is too big — the growing fields, the houses — too far away to touch.

Hrethel endured sorrow-tides for Herebald;
his score couldn't be settled, and Hæthcyn

became a stranger to his father. Hrethel lost all joy in life

and turned to the light of God; he left his hall, his home,
his heritage to his sons that survived — for all the joy
they had in it — and turned away.

Then the real bloodshed began. The sea between Swedes and Geats
ran red; we held fury between us. Ongentheow's sons tossed the feud
between them, no friendships could hold.

The hill of Hreosna was a lightning-rod to slaughter.
We matched them blow for blow, and Hæthcyn marked a final tally —

his kinsman paid his killer in steel. Eofer split Ongentheow's helmet
and the head inside it; he fell pale and silent on the hill.
Our hands did not falter. I paid Hygelac the same way:

he gave me a path in gold, I marked its miles with my blade.
The map was good; we never looked elsewhere. I was first

into battle and I'll remain so, as long as my sword and footing hold.
So it's been since the beginning, since Dæghrefn fell in front of me.
I didn't need an edge then; his heart stopped from my battle-grip,

crushing his bone-house. Now my hand must do,
one last time. I fought as a boy, as a man — and I'll fight
as an old guardian, if this dragon dares to meet me!

Sun and sea, hear the last boast of a hero, mark this

as a day worth watching. Once I tore Grendel limb from limb.
If these hands were fireproof, I'd risk them against dragon-flame,
but his venom requires a more potent antidote.

Iron shield and mail-coat must do. The dragon will be granted
no retreat and no quarter; there is one life
in the balance between us two, and darkness

lies waiting for whoever fate turns against. These words are enough:
I scream them at the sky that supports this monster;
this day will be remembered. Watch and lay witness,

which of us weathers our wounds. This is my fight:
I lay hands to it. Either I claim the hoard
and its keeper, or battle claims me.

DRAGON FLAME

Beowulf stood with his shield, brave and sure under his helmet,
and crossed towards the cliff. He knew his own strength:
this was not the path of a coward. He had fought countless battles,
he had seen blood burst like waves against a cliff-face
and come away to speak of it. Beowulf saw an arch in the stone
spitting out a boiling stream, steaming angrily in the open air.
He couldn't stay, for heat and threat of dragon-flame.
His chest swelled — Beowulf's words came in a battle-shout,
his challenge echoing against the cliff.

The dragon heard him, recognised with hatred
the sound of a man's voice. This was no time for peace.
The monster exhaled steam out of the stone;
the earth seemed to snarl. Beowulf swung his shield
against the stranger; the dragon's heart burned in angry joy.
Beowulf drew his sword, heirloom-edge
aiming sharp eyes towards the coming battle.
Each knew this went to the end — inside, each was afraid.
Beowulf stood under his shield, unyielding;
the dragon knotting and unknotting, a hand flexing for a fist,
fingers itching at a bowstring, a burning arrow.
It went in flame to meet fate.

Beowulf's shield held even shorter than he hoped; this was the first,
the only time he was not marked for victory. His sword-hand raised,
he struck at the beast, shielded in the terrible markings of its scales,

but the blade failed and glanced away; its teeth found no purchase.
The guardian of the barrow felt it and snarled, growling fire
to battle-light. There was no victory here — for Beowulf,
the journey from this world to the next would be a hard one,
the steps slow and unwillingly taken.

The terrible one came again. The dragon's breast heaved with hope:
Beowulf, the leader of his people, stood wrapped in flame.
His companions fled to the woods, hiding, terrified for their lives.
Only one's grief burned to a stronger forging — only WIGLAF,
WEOHSTAN's son, could not toss aside the claims of kinship and run.
He saw Beowulf in the crucible of his helm, burning, and remembered
the favour he bestowed — the wealthy hall of WÆGMUNDING,
land-rights given to his father before him. He could not hold back,
much as his arm might quake — it would draw his sword,
his shoulder bear his yellow shield.

BRANDING

The sword was the legacy of EANMUND, Othere's son, who died alone
at the hands of Weohstan. He bore it to Eanmund's kin,
a sword returned by sword, but Onela refused it and gave it back,
the burnished cap and mail-coat. He didn't mention the feud,
the death that brought Weohstan with death-gifts to his hall,
though Weohstan killed his brother's son. They passed to Weohstan
and his son became their keeper, hoping he might bear fruit
as noble as his father's. This would be his first test.
His spirit would hold unmelting; his father's sword defied failure.
The dragon, fire-filled on the battle-field, would find that out.

THE LAST BATTLE

But I am ahead of myself — I grow impatient for the dragon's death
and tell the punchline wrong — we are not to the death-blow yet;
we are with Wiglaf, feet shaking but sure on the ground, calling
to his comrades.
      I remember long nights in the mead-hall,
when we promised our lord we were worth the gifts he gave us,
we would repay him in our time. He chose us — he plucked us out
and raised us to his table; he saw the strength in our arms.
He wanted to take this alone, our shepherd in a last dark valley.

Now he needs us — we should go to him, help him through the flames.
By God, I would rather cover myself with that fiery blanket
than return white and unmarred, carrying my clean shield home.
I am not fit to hold it unless I can bear it in defence of Beowulf
against that monster. The deeds he has done deserve better
than fighting and falling alone. We must share it with him —
our battle-coats will shield us, our swords will aim together.

He crossed to Beowulf, stumbling in thick smoke. *When I was a boy,*
you swore that while you lived your name wouldn't leave our lips.
It has been my battle-cry since I could lift a sword — I am behind you,
to my last breath. As he spoke the serpent came.

Fire hissed a warning, burning his shield up to its boss. Wiglaf's armor
was no good. He tossed his shield aside, hid under his kinsman's,
refusing to leave the fight. Beowulf saw Wiglaf's gaze and struck,

his entire arm behind it — and *Nailing* shattered, the ancient iron
failed at last.
Weapons were often useless to Beowulf; his hand
broke strongest steel. The fire-drake saw and rushed a third time.
Fate looked at Beowulf and closed Her eyes:
the dragon's teeth sank into his neck; blood poured out, a red sea.

Wiglaf saw the death-blow beside him and proved what man he was.
He left the head with its terrible grip alone, but struck lower —
his sword-hand burning by the dragon's head — into its belly,
sinking his blade until flames drew back.
Beowulf came to, grabbed a knife from his corslet,
and dealt the final death-blow. The dragon fell, lifeless —
they had killed it together. It was Beowulf's last victory.

The dragon-bite burned, venom sinking in; Beowulf felt it
finding the path to his heart. He staggered to a seat
with the barrow before him, holding its silence inside.
Wiglaf washed his wounds, dirt and sweat caked to his helmet,
his blood-stained hands. Beowulf held a hand to his throat,
struggling to speak; he knew his book of days was closing.

I would pass this armor onto an heir, a son ready to take up his father's sword.
I have none. I ruled fifty years unchallenged — not one of our neighbors
dared risking my anger. I have stood my ground, I have kept to myself —
I have not stoked quarrels, or sworn oaths
with my fingers crossed. I feel myself dying and I'm glad of it —
I can face God with a clear conscience and squared accounts.
The dragon lies dead — Wiglaf, show me what I have died for.

Show me the treasure I leave behind, to soften the pain of my passing.

I heard Wiglaf did as he said, laying armfuls of gold out in the sun,
jewels scattering, flowers in grass, precious goblets tarnished
from the dragon's careless keeping. There were rusted helmets,
and arm-rings twisted with skills long since forgotten.
Gold in the ground, once planted, flowers slowly at any other hand.
Bright standards hung high in the hoard — they formed their own
                                        light,
bouncing quick-fingered warp and weft, shining on the treasure.

There was no trace of the dragon here — their swords
scooped him out of this world, and nothing mourned him.
And so, as I've heard, the hoard was plundered:
the cups and dishes, the standard with its impenetrable light.
Beowulf's blade had done its worst, and the treasure-protector
lost the nest egg he incubated in flame. Wiglaf hurried, impatient
for fresh air and the sight of Beowulf, breathing. He found him,
his wounds reopened. Wiglaf cleaned the blood away
as Beowulf saw the gold.
                *Thank God for this, thank God
that I set my death warrant so high. Wiglaf, you must watch
over my people; I pay for this with my life. I cannot stay.
Build me a barrow at the headland, after the sea winds
cool my funeral fire. It will tower against the sky at Hronesnæsse
as a memorial for my people; seafarers will know it,
will call it Beowulf's Barrow; they will steer by its shadow
when they come on shrouded waves.*

Beowulf took off his golden torque,
told Wiglaf to take it with his helm and mailcoat, to use them well:
You are the last of the Wægmundings now.
Fate took my kinsmen, swept every last warrior away. Now I must follow.
Those were the last words he spoke, his body
already waiting for the pyre. His breath slowed,
and stopped. Beowulf's soul left his breast in glory.

Wiglaf sat, wretchedly alone, by the body. Beowulf's slayer was near,
the serpent unwound in death. Iron edges had clipped his wings;
he fell by the house he defended. He would not glory in flight;
he fell by Beowulf's hand. Few men would hold their ground
against his venomous onslaughts, or risk pilfering his barrow,
for fear of finding him awake and angry.
Beowulf's death had been paid for; their paths had ended here.

Not long after — though late to the fight — the warriors from the
                                        woods
crept out. Ten men, clasped together like worrying, empty hands,
who failed to raise their swords in defence of their own lord.
They went ashamed in great shields and battle-dress
to where Beowulf lay. Wiglaf sat exhausted, trying to rouse him.
As much as he prayed, God had decided,
and Beowulf would not wake again. Wiglaf had grim words.

Let me be blunt. Beowulf gave you treasure, the armor
that you stand in. How many nights did we spend passing helms
and mailcoats from his ale-bench down to us in the hall?
He should have thrown that war-garb away,

for all you have done with it. He didn't need us;
God gave him arms enough when he needed his courage.
I was useless, a garnish for the dragon, but weak as I was,
I struck him, and his fire dampened. Beowulf needed us,
and in that evil moment he was almost alone.
You have had the last of your gifts —
no more swords and treasures, no more rights to your tracts of land.
You ran away like cowards, and every lord will hear it.
The men of your family will be cast out to wander in your footsteps;
death would be better than a life like that, lived in shame.

Wiglaf ordered Beowulf's victory told to the men
camped on the sea-cliff, wondering if this was Beowulf's last day,
if he would return to them. The man who rode to the headland
bore it bravely, but he brought heavy news.

THE HERALD

Our ring-giver is gone. The serpent sent him to his deathbed,
but not alone: Beowulf lies with the dragon beside him,
a great knife-wound in its belly. No sword could kill it.
Wiglaf sits at Beowulf's side, a sorrowful sentry over them.

Now we wait for war — the Franks and Frisians will hear;
they have been waiting for it. Since Hygelac came to Frisia
in the prow of a war-ship, where the Hetware attacked
and brought him low — after that, no mercy comes from there.

Nor from Sweden — after Ongentheow slaughtered Hæthcyn,
Hrethel's son, after the Geats attacked Scylfings in their arrogance.
Ohther's father answered quickly, cutting down the sea-king
and rescuing his wife, the mother of Onela and Othere, long since

stripped of her gold and ornaments. He drove his enemies out
until they scrambled to Hrefnesholt without their lord. He besieged
what swordsmen were left, wounded and weary, the entire night
he threatened, how morning would light the insides of their bodies

cut to pieces, how they would hang off gallow-trees for birds to eat.
But at first light, their grief found comfort. Hygelac's trumpet called
as he and his band of rescuers came to find them. The trail of blood
between us is a broad one, the wounds we cut into each other gape.

Ongentheow retreated with his kinsmen, made for higher ground;

Hygelac's fighting strength was well known, and he didn't trust
that he could fight off the seafaring warriors, or defend his wife
and children He drew back behind the earthen ramparts.

Hygelac came: soon enough his standard flew over the walls,
Ongentheow's refuge was overrun. He was taken, an old man brought
in a ring of swords, to Eofer — his fate was in Eofer's hands.
WULF, WONRED's son, struck at him, so that his blood sprang out,

a red tonsure against his white hair. The old king was not afraid,
but repaid him with interest. Wulf had no return blow to give,
he was cut through to hair and bone. Wulf fell bloody at that battle
but wasn't fated to die — as broken as he was, he would live.

Eofer took his place; he swung through Ongentheow's shield
to the great helm beneath it. No man could survive that blow.
Then men flew to rescue Wulf and bind his wounds, while the body
was plundered — the hard sword-hilt and helm, the corslet Eofer

brought on bent knee to Hygelac, who promised to reward him
and kept his word; once they returned home, they were granted
lands and linked rings beyond counting — and better than that,
he gave Eofer his only daughter, an honour and a blood-bond.

That is the history of our hatred, and it is why the Swedes will rejoice
as soon as they hear our lord is lifeless. When we were alone,
all our heroes fallen, he held our land against all enemies.
His deeds will be beyond telling. But even now, they come.

Now we should hurry to look at our king one last time, help him
on his way to the pyre. The gold goes with him — a grim purchase.
Let it melt with his flesh. No warrior will wear this treasure,
no beautiful maiden watch its shining jewels reflect her face.

But all of us, sorrowing, stripped of our prized possession,
must wander foreign paths now our lord has laid aside all laughter,
all gladness, all joy. Our hands will grasp for spear-shafts cold
in morning chill; no harp will resound to awaken us, but the raven,

swooping eagerly towards the stinking battlefield will tell the eagle
how it fought with wolves for our carrion, how it fared at the feast.

WITNESS

The man had hateful tidings, but he did not lie.
The company went cheerless with welling tears,
to see the last wonder of their lives. They found Beowulf
lifeless, the sand cradling him. His last day had come.
Next to him was the dragon, terrible in its scorched markings
and stench of flame, stretching for fifty feet.

It had rejoiced in dark flight; now death held it. Vessels and flagons,
wide plates and swords, lay on the earth eaten through,
longing for the ground they lived in. That legacy slept spell-bound —
no man could touch it unless God himself,
the true giver of all victories, decided he was fit to open the hoard.

Then it was clear the treasure had come to nothing.
Its guardian had killed the best of all men, settled their feud.
A man, no matter how famous, never knows
when his allotted life is over, when his space in the hall
must be taken. Even Beowulf, facing the barrow-guardian,
didn't know how his parting came.

FUNERAL

Men like us often suffer at the will of one.
As much as Beowulf loved us, he wouldn't listen
when we begged him not to attack the dragon alone,
to let it hide in its hoard until the end of the world.

The barrow stands open to all comers now. I have seen its treasure
strewn on the dirt, carried it overflowing in my hands.
He saw it before he died. He bids us build him a barrow
over his pyre, a monument as renowned as his kingship.

We saw the jewels a second time, wonders under the wall —
I will guide you. After we returned, we carried our king
to where he must stay. To build a pyre worthy of him,
the coast will be a fire-break until all our lives are forgotten.

Flame will draw the dark around him. I have seen him stand
under a sky grown black with arrows, enduring under shield-wall
shafts eager in flight, feathers straight behind singing barbs.
We sing his death now. We went under the hill for his *weregild*,

checked dark corners for the last golden scraps. No one mourned
to see those treasures plundered; none of our hands hesitated.
We pushed the dragon over the cliff, let the waves pummel its body
and pull it out to sea. The gold went onto the wagon and our king,
our grey-haired warrior, went with it to Hronesnæsse.

THE PYRE

The pyre stood ready. We hung it round with mail-coats,
battle-shields, bright helms shining back the sea.
We laid Beowulf among them, mourning our lord.
The funeral fire kindled: woodsmoke curled black
around the blaze, flames roared over our weeping
until they destroyed the bone-house, burned out his heart.

THE GEAT WOMAN

His body hidden in flames, the crackle
and puff as the center collapses —
this is when words fail, this is how they die.
My sobs, the wailing of an animal, wounded,
looking for undergrowth to hide.

What would I say? The armies will come,
captivity will stop my mouth — our lives
on a spear-point, in a merchant's purse —
long before fire's peaceful eyes turn to me.
Heaven, swallow this smoke.

THE RUIN

They built a shelter on the headland,
broad and high, visible from tides upon tides out to sea.
In ten days the monument was finished. Walls stood around it;
rings and jewels were buried in the ashes. They sleep there still,
gold gone to ground, as useless to men as it ever was.

Twelve warriors rode round the burial mound, mourning.
They sang of Beowulf and his deeds, his nobility and bravery,
a fitting tribute for any man. The Geats mourned their lord's fall,
saying that out of all kings he was the kindest and most gracious,
the gentlest to his people; and above all things, most eager for fame.